QUESTIONS ARE THE ANSWER

*nakedpastor and the search
for understanding*

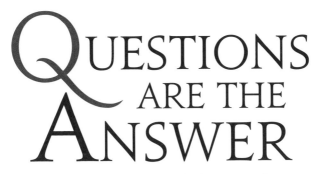

QUESTIONS ARE THE ANSWER

*nakedpastor and the search
for understanding*

DAVID HAYWARD

DARTON · LONGMAN + TODD

First published in 2015 by
Darton, Longman and Todd Ltd
1 Spencer Court
140–142 Wandsworth High Street
London SW18 4JJ

ISBN 978-0-232-53188-6

A catalogue record for this book is available from the British Library.

Designed and produced by Judy Linard
Printed and bound by Imak Ofset, Turkey

"Philosophy is not here to provide all of the answers. What it can do however, which is more powerful, is ask the right questions."
Slavoj Žižek

"... I would like to beg you dear Sir, as well as I can, to have patience with everything unresolved in your heart and to try to love the questions themselves as if they were locked rooms or books written in a very foreign language. Don't search for the answers, which could not be given to you now, because you would not be able to live them. And the point is to live everything. Live the questions now. Perhaps then, someday far in the future, you will gradually, without even noticing it, live your way into the answer."
Rainer Maria Rilke

CONTENTS

IF JESUS IS THE ANSWER, WHY'D HE HAVE SO MANY QUESTIONS?
Do you believe I can do this?
What are you guys talking about?
Who is my mother? Who are my brothers?
Anything to eat?
Who do people say that I am?
How does this concern of yours affect me?
Do you not yet understand?
Do you also want to leave me?
How long must I endure you?
Woman, where are your accusers?
What do you want me to do?
Have I been with you so long and you still don't know me?
Why do you make trouble for the woman?
Who just touched me?
Do you love me?
Why did you hit me?
Why were you looking for me?
Judas... with a kiss?
How do you read the law?
My God, my God, why have you forsaken me?
Who appointed me as your judge?

INTRODUCTION

*"Man has analyzed himself for thousands
of years, and produced no result
but literature."*
KRISHNAMURTI,
The Urgency of Change

I am just a boy sitting on the floor in a large Sunday school room in an old church. We were given an assignment to draw a picture of the bible story that the teacher just told. It was about the Hebrew people crossing the Red Sea with the Egyptian army in hot pursuit. I already loved to draw, so this was something I was happy to do. I still see that large sheet of paper on the floor in front of me. I also see a man in robes sitting beside a woman. I suppose the woman was my teacher and the man was the priest. I remember the feeling of satisfaction as I sketched and colored the scene I saw in my mind. I drew with great drama the Egyptian army drowning in the Red Sea, horses with wild eyes and men with desperate faces sinking to the muddy bottom under the weight of their sinful armor. There were blood and bubbles and beasts and brine because their deserved death had to be a horrible one.

JESUS QUESTIONS THE ELDERS

I looked up to see the priest and woman looking at me with concern. I now think it might have been a mixture of wonder and concern … wonder because it might have been a decent drawing for a boy my age, and concern because it was so brutal a depiction of the biblical story. I recall the look on their faces and that I turned back to my artwork. I was a little embarrassed but also a little stubborn. This is how it was drawn and it was too late to change it just to satisfy them! I looked up at them again and they were whispering to one another and looking at me while they were talking. I was being analyzed and I knew it.

This is my very first memory of me as an artist. It is important to me because it seems to serve as a prophecy

of things to come. I've always drawn in my own way, with as honest a self-expression as I dared. Maybe the teacher and priest might have wanted to tell me that even though it was a decent picture, perhaps it was too direct, too candid, too honest. I also still know what it means to put my work out there and have it and me analyzed as a result. I draw something I think is true, and others analyze my art with interest and concern and draw conclusions about me. There exists within me this tension between not wanting to draw attention to myself but doing the things that accomplish exactly that.

I find it strange how that little boy is still alive and well within me. I continue drawing what I want,

but under constant fear of it or me being analyzed. Yet I'm still driven to draw. I'm still impelled to see things my way and depict them as I imagine them. In spite of my own fear, I can't help being candid, direct, and honest.

HEY MOM AND DAD. I'VE DECIDED TO DISCOVER AND WALK MY OWN SPIRITUAL PATH.

I suppose I've always been a religious person. Or do I mean spiritual? Let's say I've always been interested in spiritual things and religion. I was baptized when I was a baby. But I got baptized again as a teenager when I really got saved. A few years later my family switched to another church. This is where I spent the rest of my youth. I then went to a Bible College in Springfield, Missouri, where I met my wife, Lisa. After I graduated we got married. From there we moved to Boston where I earned my Masters in Theological Studies. After I graduated I became an assistant minister in a larger Presbyterian church in Canada for three years. When I finished there

QUESTIONS ARE THE ANSWER

I went to McGill University where I earned my Diploma in Ministry. I was ordained and served various kinds of churches as a pastor until 2010. But, in March of 2010, I suddenly realized I was finished. I knew beyond a shadow of a doubt that my days as a pastor were complete and I left the ministry immediately. I haven't been a member of a church since.

I have visited some churches and have even spoken at a few. But since 2010 I have not been a part of the institutional church. More of the juicy details will emerge during the telling of my story. Much of my writing and many of my cartoons issue from this very intense journey I am about to share with you.

INTRODUCTION

I've drawn many cartoons on the subject of questions and their value. Most of them are in this book. Questions not only open the door for answers, they also open the door to mystery and trouble. In fact, as many of these cartoons depict, asking too many questions or the wrong kinds of questions can get you into plenty of difficulty. So over the course of time I eventually came to detect that there are three stages of questions that I've journeyed through.

I picture a door on a hinge. The door is closed, swinging, or open. Like questions!

The first kind of questions is closed questions. The answer to these questions is a simple yes *or* no. There are no other options but these two. It's a very black and white world with no grays or shadows in between. It's one or the other. I would characterize this period as a time of certainty and conformity.

The second kind of questions is swinging questions. The answer to these questions is yes *and* no. There are two options. Or maybe there's another one we haven't even considered yet. It's still a fairly black and white world, but this world is getting more complicated with grays and shadows in between. I would characterize this period as a time of confusion.

The third kind of questions is open questions. The answer to these questions is that there isn't an answer. Oh, there may be an answer, but we don't know what it is, we don't pretend that there is, and we remain open in order to discern it when or if it should arrive. I would characterize this period as a time of contentment.

This is my journey through these stages of questioning. Even though we may revisit the different kinds of questions at different times in our lives, I see these stages as delineating different passages of my spiritual journey. Closed questions represent my immature spirituality. Swinging questions typified my growing spirituality. Open questions belong to my more mature spirituality.

I am not totally pleased with the word "stage". These aren't really places, but ways of seeing. Reality is not in the future waiting for us to catch up and arrive. It is here all the time, giving us clues to its truth if only we would see and embrace it. So, it is not reality's elusiveness, but

our resistance to it that is the problem. When I observe myself, I can say that I have been very reluctant to see throughout my life. I'm a slow learner. The clues were always there, but it took time to detect and then follow them to where they were leading me. This is the journey I want to talk about.

I hope you enjoy the journey with me. Some of the cartoons may be funny. Some may be angry. Some may be poignant. But I hope they all provide a little scenery along the inquisitive path my story leads you down.

Right from the beginning, though, I want to give a kind of disclaimer. One of my favorite writers, Wendell Berry, says it best, so I'll just quote him:

QUESTIONS ARE THE ANSWER

"But it's awfully hard, when you write arguments, to avoid the tone that implies that you know what other people ought to do. My work is best, I think, when I talk as a person who's not an authority on anything but his own experience."

(Grubbs, *Conversations with Wendell Berry*)

This is about my own experience.

CHAPTER ONE
CLOSED QUESTIONS

*"I know you won't believe me, but the
highest form of human excellence
is to question oneself and others."*
Socrates

There's a bible I've kept since I was a teenager in youth group. Our youth leader was a schoolteacher, Bruce. He was really cool, and we all thought his wife was gorgeous. I couldn't wait for all the youth to go to his house so I could study the bible and look at his wife. For some reason Bruce took me under his wing. He must have noticed my keenness for the bible.

He bought me a Parallel Bible with 4 versions of the New Testament running side by side. Many times he would invite me over to study it with him. We would have our colored pencils and pens and read each verse and talk about them in detail. We completed whole chunks

of the New Testament this way. That bible is marked to smithereens, full of color, explanations and exclamations.

Bruce was radical. He took the bible literally and taught me to as well. This got him into trouble with the pastor. I suppose Bruce didn't feel the pastor was biblical enough or faithful enough to scripture. I'm not sure what the issues were, but I know they had something to do with Bruce's bible-fueled radicalism clashing with the pastor's idea of what a church and a Christian should be. I got the impression Bruce was being edged out of the church. It wasn't long until he and his wife moved away to teach at another school.

My family soon switched to another church.

I didn't have much of a social life outside of the church. The youth groups were very active. That kept me busy. Not in an unhappy way. I enjoyed it. They were rather large groups. We listened to contemporary Jesus music. That was cool.

We formed friendships that, in a small town, transferred into our high schools. I was musical so I was a part of a Christian music band and we travelled around to other youth groups. We would study the bible together. We considered ourselves radical Christians and probably truer Christians because, unlike other youth groups that held relevant talks and endless games and activities, we just studied the bible. My life was busy with Sunday morning and evening services, mid-week bible studies,

JESUS IS THE

©nakedpastor

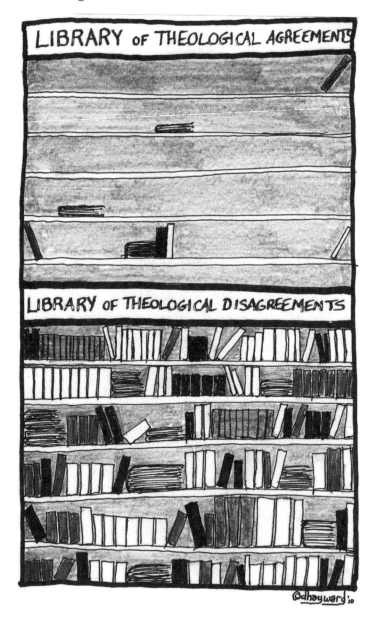

youth group, Sunday school, and music groups. I also studied the bible on my own as much as I could.

There were also a lot of books in our house. So I not only spent my spare time with music and drawing, but also reading. They were from a very conservative and orthodox viewpoint, and they all fed into my very structured theological world.

My universe was very black and white. Later, after reading James Fowler's *Stages of Faith*, I would appreciate this very certain stage of conformity. Only a few things disturbed this orderly, dualistic world at such a young age.

One was a friend, whom I loved very much, who wasn't sure she believed in a God who would allow her family to split up the way it did. How could such a beautiful and sad person be sent to Hell when it wasn't her fault? Another was asking the pastor of my church, whom I thought was very cool, if he could speak to us about premarital sex. We know the bible says it's wrong. But why is it wrong? I found it strange that he couldn't or wouldn't answer that. But I learned to ignore these disturbing questions that conflicted with my beliefs. As Fowler says, it was because I feared the threat these inconsistencies would introduce to my very structured world.

When I graduated from high school, I eventually went to a Bible College in Springfield, Missouri, as a music major. Even though the religious culture there was

very black and white, I was pretty much on the periphery of it for the first three years studying music.

Then I met Lisa.

We fell in love. It wasn't long until we had a conversation about our future. It was obvious to both of us that we wanted to spend the rest of our lives together. But after one Friday night chapel service, she said something like this to me: "I don't know how we're going to do this. I want to be a missionary and you want to be a music minister in a church. I can't see how this is going to work!"

Being madly in love and wanting to be with her forever, I quickly renegotiated my future. I decided I

CLOSED QUESTIONS

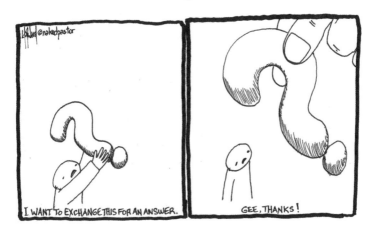

would transfer out of the music program and into Bible and Theology. My parents were supportive, which was all I needed to make the final leap and switch majors. This is where I came under the tutelage of some bible scholars. They opened up whole new depths for me. It wasn't totally new to me. This new line of studies tapped into my deep and lasting love for scripture, and I excelled. I took two years of Greek and a year of Hebrew, along with studying books and letters of the bible. I fell even more deeply in love with it.

QUESTIONS ARE THE ANSWER

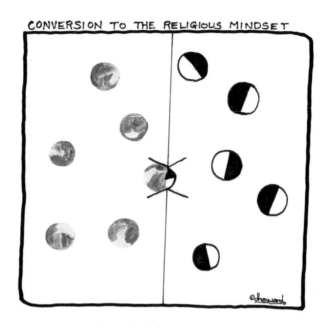

CLOSED QUESTIONS

After I graduated, Lisa and I got married and moved to Boston where I attended Gordon-Conwell Theological Seminary to study my Masters in Bible and Theology. I was fortunate to be mentored by some of the most influential biblical theologians. I studied more Greek, more Hebrew, Aramaic, and the texts of the New Testament. This seminary was on the cutting edge of conservative Christianity, but it was still very conservative.

Even though my world was very black and white, at the time it felt very ordered and beautiful. I was happy in it.

Then, just before my graduation, I read *The Silence of Jesus: The Authentic Voice of the Historical Man*, by James Breech. I don't know why I read it. Perhaps a friend

BIBLE BUNKER

showed it to me. Or maybe I saw it in the bookstore. I don't think it would have been required reading because it certainly wasn't from the seminary's theological perspective. Breech's argument is that there are essentially a few sayings of Jesus that could be relied upon as authentic. He proceeds to analyze these through a very convincing critical lens. As I was reading it, I could feel the foundations of my theological earth move.

Everything, my whole life, suddenly became very unstable and terrifying.

My parents were visiting from Toronto, and Lisa's parents and grandmother were visiting from Alabama.

We were all stuffed into our tiny one-bedroom apartment getting ready to go to my graduation ceremony. I was literally freaking out. Everything I ever believed was in crisis! It was like I had a tidy sturdy stack of blocks and one of the bottom ones supporting the whole stack … the inspiration and infallibility of scripture … had been pulled out.

CLOSED QUESTIONS

I could feel absolutely everything about my world getting ready to crumble into a confusing and complicated heap. Lisa literally grabbed me and shook me and told me to calm down and that I had to get it together because I was graduating in just one hour. Somehow it jolted me out of my panic and I calmed down enough to go through the motions of my graduation.

Another significant incident happened at seminary. One of my favorite New Testament professors was dismissed for suggesting that the words of Jesus and John the Baptist recorded in the gospels may not have occurred, and that Jesus' self-knowledge about his divinity developed over his lifetime. I was so confused over this and sad for my professor. It was frightening because

QUESTIONS ARE THE ANSWER

I now realized that there are serious ramifications for questioning orthodox or popularly held interpretations of the bible or questioning its infallibility.

My peace was broken. The damage was done. My neatly ordered world was no longer black and white. I was about to enter the longest and darkest part of my journey.

CHAPTER TWO
SWINGING QUESTIONS

The church's specialty "*has always been*
the neutralization of the overly curious
mind through faith"
the cardinal,
Death With Interruptions, José Saramago

Toward the end of my seminary days, I realized that finding employment in the kind of church I was used to probably wouldn't happen. I put out some resumés but nothing came back. A fellow student of mine who also happened to be my neighbor suggested I apply to a more mainline church in Canada. They were looking for an assistant to the minister. After a series of meetings and interviews, I got the job.

The first year went pretty well. It was a large city church and had a lot of youth. It kept me very busy, along with some preaching and teaching, Sunday school, youth groups, visitation, and charity work.

SWINGING QUESTIONS

I read a bunch of books about personal responsibility and organization ... one-minute manager kind of stuff. This was my attempt to inject some order and discipline into my insanely busy life as an assistant pastor of a fair-sized church. I strategized my life down to fifteen-minute intervals. Yes, I know. Anal!

As a result, I spent a lot of my time studying the Greek and Hebrew texts of the bible, reading theology, preparing teachings, visiting the sick and elderly, and handing out food to people who came in off the street. The minister was conservative, so it helped me stay within the fold of conservative theology during that time. I think it somehow forestalled my clear-cut departure from my black and white world. Even though my confidence in the inspiration and

@nakedpastor

infallibility of scripture had been undermined, I somehow put that to the back of my mind. It certainly was easier to be myself here than where I used to be, and I appreciated that. I was doing very well with the youth group growing and people enjoying my teaching.

But something was about to change all that.

I was at the church studying on a winter's day. There was a huge snowstorm forecast and it had begun. It was getting close to 5pm. I was collecting my things to go home before the full storm arrived, when the secretary called me on the intercom: "David. Could you please come to the office? There's a street person in the lobby and he's scaring me." I was so frustrated by this that I told her just to give him some food and send him away. She said she was too frightened to leave her office. So I slammed down my bible and stomped out to the lobby.

There he was, a gruff, old man in dirty, worn out clothes and obviously inebriated. I slid my arm around his shoulder and started escorting him to the door. He said, "You wouldn't give a poor fella some food, would ya?"

I said, "You come back sober and we'll talk business!"

"Oh, come on! Just give me a bit of food would'ya?" he asked.

"You come back sober and we'll talk," I said, all the while edging him closer to the exit. I opened the huge wooden doors and a blast of cold air and snow blew in.

One more time, he begged, "Please! Just a little food for a poor fella!"

"Oh Lord, I would like to see the whole world saved!"

"Oh! Wow! Thanks!"

I gently nudged him out onto the steps and said, again, "You come back when you're sober and we'll talk business!"

He stumbled down the snowy steps, and just when I was about to shut the door on him he turned around, looked me straight in the eye, and in as sober a voice as I've ever heard, he said, "You'll NEVER be a minister the way you treated me!" He then disappeared into the white storm never to be seen by me again.

Those words, like no other words ever, pierced me straight through to the heart. I let the door close and I rushed back to my office. I heard the secretary eventually leave. I knew I had to go soon or I'd get stuck in the storm. But once I knew I was alone, I laid my head on my arms on my desk, and wept. It was an uncontrollable sobbing. I was devastated. Completely undone!

I packed up my stuff and made it to my car and drove out into the country where Lisa was waiting for me at our tiny home. I cried all the way there. When I got there she asked what was wrong. I tried to tell her. Now, the story itself isn't all that much. Like so many of us do when we're in a hurry, I brushed a street person off. But it was what it *meant* that devastated me. Here I was trying to live a disciplined life, studying the bible, as a pastor, and in a church. Here I was confronted with a person in obvious need. Somehow it exposed the loveless emptiness of my heart and mind. It uncovered the fruitlessness of discipline, effort, and study to make myself a spiritual person … a better person. Lisa has often told me that the more spiritual I try to be the worse a person I become. Case in point!

My lack of trust in the infallibility of scripture as well as my own infallibility crashed into one another, creating a horrific accident scene that would take some time to investigate and untangle. I couldn't trust the bible. I couldn't trust myself. This filled me with a sense of futility and hopelessness.

Fortunately, the storm snowed us in for many days, so I had all that time to regain some sanity and regain my composure. I mean, I knew this wasn't just something I had to get over. I realized this was a significant traumatic event that was going to change me. But I was completely directionless. I had no idea what to do next.

That night a friend of mine from seminary days called. He said, "You'll never guess who I just went to listen to tonight!" I couldn't guess. I didn't even want to bother trying. Finally, he said, "Henri Nouwen! David, it changed my life! It was unbelievable! I've got the tape. I'm going to send it to you!"

After we got off the phone, I sat there thinking, "Henri Nouwen. Henri Nouwen. Where have I heard that name before?" Lisa said, "Didn't someone give you a book of Nouwen's for a graduation gift?" I wasn't sure. I had unpacked all my books, hundreds of them, and placed them on my shelves. It wasn't there. I knew I had more books in storage that I didn't care about, so I got them and looked through them. Sure enough, I found a book by Henri Nouwen called *Reaching Out:*

He is stuck inside a box. His body grew. His head did not.

QUESTIONS ARE THE ANSWER

The Three Movements of the Spiritual Life. I chuckled to myself because when my friend gave me this book as a graduation gift, I inwardly scoffed at it. I wasn't interested! I only cared about the bible and what it had to say, not any of this New Age mystical spirituality crap!

But, right now I felt so spiritually bankrupt that I decided to read it. The way this had all turned out … with the storm, the drunk, the phone call, and the book already in my possession … it felt predestined. All I did all weekend was read this book slowly. It was at this

point I also started keeping a journal. I kept notes and documented my reflections as I went through the book. It was exactly what I needed at the time.

In turn, Nouwen led me to Thomas Merton, the American Benedictine monk. I read all of his works, including his reflections on eastern philosophy and religion. Around this time I had a very vivid dream in which I saw a stained glass mask. I knew it meant that even though our religion can be very attractive and beautiful, it is still a mask that conceals the real. This disturbed me because I was so wrapped up in religion and was suddenly aware of my deep, personal issues. This compelled me to seek and find a spiritual director, a nun who was a professional spiritual director in a monastery there. I went through, as Lisa calls it, my Gandhi phase. I started reading everything I could get my hands on to do with spirituality as well as understanding the self, including Carl Jung.

"Come on God! You just HAVE to fit in there!"

I was finally being pulled out of my black and white world of either–or into the multi-shaded world of both–and. I was ushered into a new and paradoxical universe.

How my time ended at that church was interesting. I had been there three years. Lisa and I had talked about what we wanted to do: stay, or for me to go into further studies, a PhD in New Testament. We decided we would stay. One night, we were visiting the head elder and his wife. We had a nice meal and afterwards were enjoying a game of billiards. In passing, I said that Lisa and I were looking forward to what we were going to do at the church in the coming year. The elder said, "Oh! Haven't

you heard?" "No," I said, "What?" "Your contract has been discontinued. You're finished here." News to me! Lisa and I were shocked. The elders had been informed that I was going back to school. I was hurt, baffled, and angry. I thought that was unfair and unkind, but I was told what was done was done. It was then that I began to discern the role power plays in the church. I know I had changed since coming there, but I felt it was spiritual growth and that it would have a positive impact on my ministry. Obviously, not everyone agreed.

So Lisa and I did what we felt was our only choice. I went back to school. For the next couple of years I studied at the University of Toronto and McGill University and finally received my Diploma in Ministry. I fell in love with theology. I was committed!

On the eve of my ordination, I was hanging out with my friends who were being ordained with me, as well as with my friend who was already ordained and was preaching our ordination sermon. I was in such turmoil! Was I doing the right thing? I don't think it was just about the seriousness of the call. Did I intuitively sense I was walking into what I wouldn't realize was a trap until almost a quarter of a century later? Did I sense the dualistic nature of my sense of call, or that I was predicting the ambiguous aspects of my vocation as a pastor?

A few years later I read Furlong's insights about the Benedictine monk Thomas Merton:

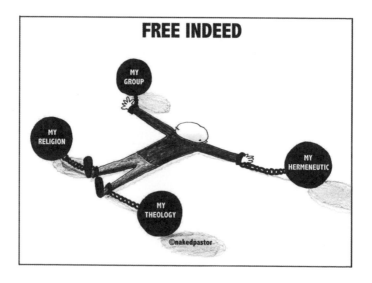

"...*those who believed themselves to have a vocation, a call, needed to reach a stage in their development when they knew that the constraint had not been quite of the kind they originally thought, but rather an inevitable outcome of their temperament, upbringing, and the particular problems they had.*"

(Furlong, *Merton*)

I was so confused and conflicted. My friends were getting exasperated with me and advised me that it was just nerves and to just do it. So I did. In 1988 I got ordained.

QUESTIONS ARE THE ANSWER

Over the next six years our three children were born. I served smaller churches, so I had a lot of time to study, think, and write in my journal. It was a time of both intense personal, spiritual and intellectual growth, but also a time of intense personal, spiritual and intellectual confusion, angst, and struggle.

This is the nature of this second stage of questioning. They are no longer black and white, either–or, and yes–no questions. On the one hand, I still cherished the bible and my theology. It seemed true to me. But on the other hand, I had this new spiritual openness dawning within me that also seemed true. The bible seemed clear about so many things. But these were being challenged by my new discoveries about myself as well as spiritual realities I was discovering through my own thoughts, meditations, revelations, and readings.

The anguish I suffered during these years was sometimes unbearable. I had frequent headaches, was

©nakedpastor

always fatigued, and often felt dishonest in my sermons. The dishonesty wasn't that I was lying. It was that I really didn't know the answer but felt I had to still show confidence in the pulpit. I didn't know the full truth. As a result, like so many pastors, I sounded more certain than I actually was.

Having studied Jung and other writers concerned with inner work, I was under enormous pressure to be a person of integrity. I saw spiritual directors and therapists and counselors. I did lots of meditation, self-analysis and reflection. I did a ton of reading and studying. I wrote a lot in my journals. I fell in love with reformed theologians like Barth, and also fell in love with eastern philosophers like Krishnamurti. How can this be? How can one reconcile these two extremes?

One story typifies my struggle during this time. I used to go to a nearby town to visit the university's library. I would find abstracts and journal articles on various spiritual, psychological, and philosophical topics, and I took extensive notes. I would meet up with a friend and we would discuss our recent readings. He asked me what I was reading, so I told him I was reading Krishnamurti's, *The Urgency of Change*, and that it was a significant book for me. In fact, to this day, it is one of the most important books in my spiritual development. I shared with him a couple of quotes from the book that struck terror in my heart:

QUESTIONS ARE THE ANSWER

"You go only so far in your self-criticism. The very entity that criticizes must be criticized, must be examined."

And this one:

"Only the deep, constant demand of the brain for the physical security of the organism is inherent. Symbols are a device of the brain to protect the psyche; this is the whole process of thought. The 'me' is a symbol, not an actuality. Having created the symbol of the 'me', thought identifies itself with its conclusion, with the formula, and then defends it: all misery and sorrow come from this."

I expressed the fear these thoughts evoked in me. They rang true. But if they were true, then I was in real trouble.

©nakedpastor

He replied, in essence, "Why are you reading that stuff? Christianity has enough books of its own. Just like the bible interprets itself, so Christianity has all you need to know to understand how to be spiritual. You shouldn't be reading that Eastern stuff!" He articulated my inner guilt and shame about it. There was a part of me that agreed with him. But there was another part that resented it.

I didn't know what was true. But, somehow I knew that his assertion was wrong. I felt like it was a compromise. A cop-out.

I'd read something about Barth that stuck with me:

"'True joy is a serious matter,' and could only be found if one 'stuck to one's guns' and like the knight in Dürer's famous picture, 'between death and the devil', rode straight through the hostile fronts of the present day. It was no use looking for some tedious compromise; a breakthrough was the only answer."

(Busch, *Karl Barth: His Life from Letters and Autobiographical Texts*)

I couldn't compromise. I couldn't quit. I needed this breakthrough. I had to wait for it.

In 1995 I crashed. I had become frustrated and bored with being a pastor. I'd even accepted an offer to start a brand new church from scratch. I accepted it with the idea that if I started something new I could grow it into something I wanted it to be. But, after just two years it fell into the same old rut. I became entirely hopeless. In fact, looking back, I was probably depressed.

As Merton said about Jonah, I was living in the belly of a paradox. I instinctively knew that the answer wasn't choosing one side or the other of the paradoxical equation. Like Barth said, the way to wisdom is not around the problem but through it. I simply could not see my way through. I was completely in the dark. I was at the dead end of my vocation as a pastor and dead at the end of my rope spiritually. I've never felt so trapped in all my life.

All I wanted was a way to integrate these two sides of the paradox I found myself trapped between. I was passionate about theological depth but I was also passionate about personal spiritual experience. Alas, they were at odds! Generally, my observations so far proved that if we pursued theological depth we become spiritually cold, but if we pursued personal spiritual experience we become intellectually shallow.

One night I had a dream. All I heard were the words, "It's time!" I woke up laughing. My laughter awakened

Pastor Bill, very early Sunday morning, was awakened with a start from a nightmare in which, before he could enter into Heaven, he had to sign a confession admitting that what he had preached all those years was not entirely true.

Lisa and the kids. The kids came in and jumped on our bed and we were all laughing together. They asked what I was laughing about. I couldn't explain it. All I could say was that I was no longer trapped. I knew upon waking that I was free. Entirely free! All I had to do was walk away from it all.

So we did. I resigned as minister of the church, sold what we could, packed the rest in our van, and went to visit my parents in Ontario. Over the course of the next several weeks we decided to move to the little town of

Quispamsis, just outside of Saint John, New Brunswick. We moved there and started attending a church called Rothesay Vineyard. The next year the pastor went to start a new church in Ohio and left the church to me as its pastor.

What Lisa and I appreciated so much about this church was that it attempted to combine the two sides of the paradox I wrestled between: serious theology and spiritual passion. We were going to enjoy this!

I've come to the conclusion that this paradox I struggled between is full of anguish. The mind demands to settle in one place. It seems to require simplicity. It insists on certainty. The subtle dance of paradoxical thinking and living is a challenging art. I'd read about Keats' description of 'The Man of Achievement'. Solnit tells the story best:

> "*On a midwinter's night in 1817, a little over a century before Woolf's journal entry on darkness, the poet John Keats walked home talking with some friends and as he wrote in a celebrated letter describing that*

walk, 'several things dovetailed in my mind, and at once it struck me what quality went to form a Man of Achievement, especially in Literature ... I mean Negative Capability, that is, when a man is capable of being in uncertainties, mysteries, doubts, without any reaching after fact and reason."

(Rebecca Solnit, *Men Explain Things to Me*)

I wanted this quality! But how to acquire it?

Over the next many years I tried to dance this dance. I continued my study of theology. I kept reading Barth, especially his epic *The Epistle to the Romans*. He said when he wrote his Romans commentary he was like a boy who tripped in the bell tower and accidentally grabbed the rope to the bell that rang throughout the world. When I read that book, the bell indeed rang for me! I also continued reading other theologians, mystics, and writers from other religions and philosophies,

This was an extremely rich and enjoyable time of our lives. But then something was about to happen that would change all that too. Over the next decade I was going to start experiencing my disappointment in the church's inability to provide a safe space for people like me to grow theologically as well as develop spiritually in our own way. I would eventually learn that I was under the illusion of being free, but that there were limits on my freedom and therefore not free at all.

Then tragedy struck. In 1997, our church went through a massive church split that it never recovered from until its final closure in the fall of 2014. It started with me simply asking questions about such issues as the role of pastor, how communities can be healthy, about money, and about the previous pastor's influence on our church, and other taboo topics. We lost over half of the congregation in a week.

Even though I continued my search for what is true and for what does work in a healthy community, I also believed that the church was a treacherous place within which to attempt this. For those who stayed at the church following the split and didn't leave with so many of the others who did, many struggled with their own disillusionment with the church. This church had been amazing … growing, energetic, young, rich, influential, exciting, and fun. It was a great place to be. Then overnight it was all gone. The church as we knew it vanished. Now it is gone for good. Closed and sold! Some took the theologically easy route and said we were a sinful church, so they transferred to other churches

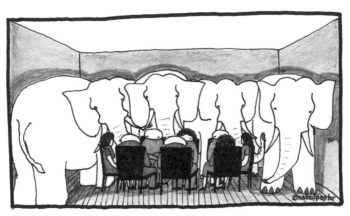

that picked up the torch where we supposedly dropped it. But, for many, they couldn't evade the conclusion that a lot of what we call church is a façade. A game. For just beneath the skin of this amazing church was a deceitful heart. We also realized that influential people can destroy a good thing in a moment. If people realized this and were willing to question it further, they would have to come to the conclusion, like I did, that this was typical of all churches and all institutions. No matter how wonderful something is it may not take much for it to turn and expose its dark side. This isn't a pessimistic posture, but a realistic one I think is necessary to hold if

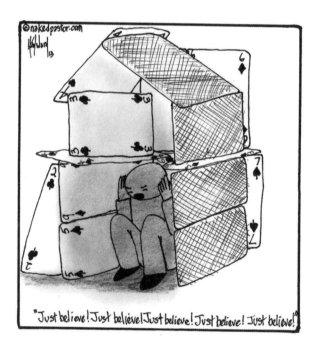

"Just believe! Just believe! Just believe! Just believe! Just believe!"

we want to affect any meaningful change. Like Richard Rohr says, "The presumption for anyone with a dualistic mind is that if you criticize something, you don't love it. Wise people like the prophets would say the opposite … The Hebrew prophets were free to love their tradition and to criticize it at the same time, which is a very rare art form." My observations are that few people are willing to acquire or appreciate that art form.

I told a friend my harrowing story of the church split, and how heartbroken I was because I really did love that church and now it was all blown to smithereens. He said, "Then, get another vision." But, I didn't want to! I'd

been searching for the church of my dreams for so long and finally found it. Not only did I find it, I was given the privilege of being its pastor! Now it was all gone. The church of my dreams was an illusion, a fantasy, a misty vision. Why even bother looking for an even better one? It was impossible. I became hopeless.

This tragedy destroyed my illusions about church and theology. For the next fifteen years the split and its ramifications motivated me to seriously explore how a community can be genuinely healthy and not just pretend to be. It also inspired me to search for what was really true.

In 2002 I left that church to my assistant and went to start a church for an international ministry in New Hampshire. It was to be a permanent change. But after just a few months I was fired for insubordination because I refused to participate in a ministry-wide repentance campaign to get rid of what they believed was sin in the camp. Of course, this relatively small incident was all that was needed to sever what had become a very difficult and disappointing experience. Our church back home and its leadership team warmly encouraged and invited us back. So we returned to our church and over the next few years recovered from the serious trauma we suffered in New Hampshire. We quietly sat in the back row. I did odd jobs for the next few years, seriously thinking that I was completely done serving the church.

This experience at an international ministry further cemented my belief that not only the church, but also all its para-church expressions are susceptible to profound dysfunction. Having been disillusioned with the church itself, I'd hoped that serving people outside of the church walls would be different, free from the complications of organized church life. But what it proved was that dysfunction happens anywhere. In fact, independent ministries can be even more dangerous because there's a complete lack of accountability. I raised questions at this ministry that were obviously irritating to its leadership. I naively assumed I was contributing to the improvement of a community and it's ministry's health because that's why I thought I was hired. Instead, I came to realize that, as with all organizations, I was employed to further its agenda, service its goals, and not get in their way. When I didn't fulfill this I was summarily dismissed.

In 2006, the pastor back home passed the church back to me so he could pursue another career. Believe

MY PERSONAL WALK WITH JESUS OVER THE YEARS

@nakedpastor

it or not, I was ready to try it again. I'd learned a lot. I firmly believed that people had the right to gather together around a commonality for worship, learning, fellowship and service. My only concern was that it be done in a healthy manner. Surely it must be possible! I was intently focused on experimenting with this idea.

I was also intent on finding what the truth was. No more nonsense! I'd drifted through so many theological streams, and all of them … their theologies and their praxis … were problematic. I'm not condemning them, because even though I eventually found them limiting, I wouldn't be where I am without having gone through them. But they did not satisfy my hunger and thirst for healthy community and honest thinking.

So I started my blog, nakedpastor, where I could bare my soul as a pastor. I challenged myself to write and draw a cartoon every day. I called myself a graffiti artist on the walls of religion. Mostly, I needed and wanted a place where I could pose my questions. I thought perhaps my inquiries would motivate and encourage others to ask their own questions too. I didn't realize how much of a plague I would become. Socrates teaches us that raising critical questions is an important and useful project.

"Socrates can be seen as a nuisance, constantly irritating others with his logical inquiries. Euthyphro handled the cross-examination with a good spirit, but not everyone did. With his questioning Socrates is a slayer of idols.

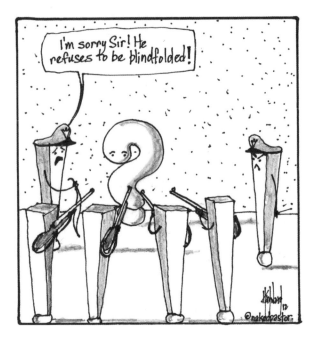

At times, nothing of a conversant's original position is left standing, as the search for truth clears away false opinions like a scythe clears away unwanted brush. All opinions must stand the test of critical examination."

(Kenneth Shouler, *The Everything Guide to Understanding Philosophy*)

Anguish is the word that would characterize my spiritual condition over these many years. This caused me to dive even deeper into my studies and into my experiments at our church to facilitate healthy community. Of course, this would lead me down what are considered treacherous theological paths. My preaching started to reflect a more inquisitive approach. We would have discussions, open questions and answer, and even debates, throughout the sermon time. For some people this was very uncomfortable, including for me when it became adversarial. But I didn't know and I was driven to know, and this required honesty in my search and collaboration with the community.

I'd read about this Abraham Lincoln:

> *"It also made for a pragmatic approach to problems, a recognition that if one solution was fated not to work another could be tried. 'My policy is to have no policy'*

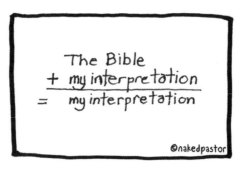

became a kind of motto for Lincoln—a motto that infuriated the sober, doctrinaire people around him who were inclined to think that the President had no principles either. He might have offended his critics less if he had more often used the analogy he gave James G. Blaine when explaining his course on Reconstruction: 'The pilots on our Western rivers steer from point to point *as they call it—setting the course of the boat no further than they can see; and that is all I propose to myself in this great problem.'"*

(Fred Kaplan, *Lincoln*)

I wasn't at my destination yet. But, like Lincoln I was determined to set my course no further than I could see and trust that we would eventually arrive where we needed to both theologically and communally.

One of the first most practical theological quandaries was over gay and lesbian people. There were a few gay and lesbian people who wanted to come to our church. I let them know they were welcomed. Some people didn't like that. They would believe "love the sinner hate the sin," but when it came down to actually being with gay and lesbian people, it got messy and complicated. Hating the sin always seems to trump loving the sinner. My theology was constantly being challenged.

A few years before this, Lisa and I went on a short vacation in Maine to meet friends there and hang out for the weekend. One evening over supper we talked about homosexuality and our gay and lesbian friends. I proposed, "love the sinner hate the sin" and my friend challenged me on the inconsistency and hypocrisy of this line of thinking. I was taken aback but it got me wondering. Later that evening we filled up our insulated cups with wine and went

to the hot tub. While we were there, three men joined us. We started talking, and they revealed that they were gay. When they found out I was a pastor, they shared their stories of being rejected from their churches, not being able to get furnace oil in the winter because no one would deliver it to them, rejection from their families, and harassment at work. It was a revelation listening to them. I thought it was fortuitous that our theological conversation over supper and this encounter should happen within hours. I took it as a sign. I forsook the "love the sinner hate the sin" and decided that I would choose love and inclusion without judgment, and that I would trust for clarity to come some time in the future, like Lincoln's river boats winding their way up a bending river.

My style of ministry was changing. It became even more democratic and collaborative. We held what we called open round tables where my fantastic leadership team would meet, and anyone could join us. They were incredibly intense but always very fruitful. I was certain that no matter how chaotic things could get, as long as we remembered we were in this together to make healthy community, then it would be a creative chaos. Also, my sermons were not monologues any more. In fact, they were no longer recognizable as sermons because they were discussions. I admitted I didn't have the answer to a lot of things. But I wanted to. These were also very intense times, but as long as we remembered that we were searching for what is true together, we could cut through the entanglements to get there together.

Not everyone appreciated it. Most people, when they go to church, want answers, not questions. They want a program, not a community. Here, they got neither answers nor programs. Over time I started getting more communications from concerned members, suggesting that perhaps I wasn't really called to be a pastor any more. Some were genuinely worried about me, that I was no longer happy, and that I needed to find something else to do. Still others were alarmed at the developments in my theology. It became very obvious very quickly that I was no longer on the same page as a growing segment of the congregation. In the past I would have done my duty and conformed to the expectations of the congregation. But

now the urgency to live an authentically integrated life both inside and out became my priority.

How did this incongruity between the congregation and me happen? Two reasons.

One is I had a dream that changed my life forever. I'll tell you more about it soon. For now, I can say that this had an immediate effect on me. It had an effect on me personally because I felt an immediate peace that has never gone away. I had a sudden clarity that has persisted and become even clearer. But this also had an effect on the way I did my job. My sermons were even more conversational and dialogical. (Some say diabolical.) My leadership style became even more open and collaborative. I was challenging myself to be more honest. The heat was turned up, and I started to feel it.

Second, my blog nakedpastor was getting more attention. The people in my congregation never used to read it. They'd jokingly say, "We have to listen to you every week! Why would we want to hear from you every day?" But, when others started noticing my material and that it seemed to them less orthodox and more irreverent, some people started talking. Some members of other churches talked to some members of my church and about me as well as my questionable theology.

I knew my cartoons and writings were controversial. Graffiti usually is. Not everyone would agree that Banksy is a graffiti artist, but I appreciate the truth he speaks to power. In the same way, I want to challenge

QUESTIONS ARE THE ANSWER

the church where it takes advantage of its privileges and abuses its power. I do recognize that I am critiquing something I love, but I always endeavor to do it in a way that contributes to exposing our unity rather than concealing it. I remember something Torrance wrote about Barth that I try to apply daily to my work:

> "*Another aspect of Barth's humanity was his irrepressible humour. What we are concerned with here is the theological significance of this, for Barth's humour played a fundamentally critical role in*

his thinking. He was able to laugh at himself, and therefore to criticize himself, and hence could direct even ruthless critique at others in such a way that he could appreciate their intentions and respect their persons and their sincerity ... he would never let himself become a prisoner of his own formulations."
(Karl Barth, *Biblical and Evangelical Theologian*)

However, in spite of my attempts to contribute to the conversation in helpful but honest ways, I guess I was becoming too problematic for too many. Eventually, the national director of our church's denomination would call me. The scrutiny was intensifying from all quarters.

Eventually, feeling the pressure from my own denomination, from other churches and Christians, and finally from many of my own members, I had to face the possibility that we were no longer compatible. Finally, in March of 2010, I decided that I was done. I would leave the ministry. It would be better for me and better for the church.

My dream as well as my departure from ministry and the organized church catapulted me suddenly and furiously into years of deconstruction, but at the same time an everlasting peace.

I can't wait to tell you about it!

CHAPTER THREE
OPEN
QUESTIONS

*"But the true 'Copernican' revolution
takes place when, instead of just adding
complications and changing minor
premises, the basic framework itself
undergoes transformation."*
Slavoj Žižek

Having struggled for so many years, I came to the conclusion that I was stuck with it. At first, this was a sad realization. However, over the next period I learned an important lesson, and it's that my goal wasn't the elimination of the difficult qualities of contradiction and confusion. Rather, it was going to be my ability to live at peace with them. As Hollis says, "Clearly, psychological or spiritual development always requires a greater capacity in us for the toleration of anxiety and ambiguity. The capacity to accept this troubled state, abide it, and commit to life, is the moral measure of our

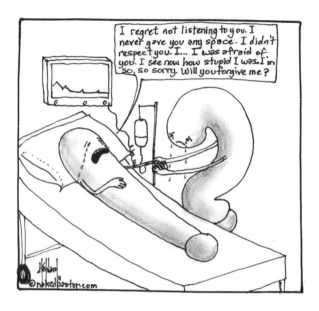

maturity." (James Hollis, *Finding Meaning in the Second Half of Life*).

This is difficult for me to talk about. Not emotionally, but intellectually. It's an experience that defies articulation. There are no words. Nevertheless, I know I must try because it is so crucial to explain my life, how I changed, and what I do now. This was my breakthrough!

It all started when I had a very simple dream on May 11, 2009. This is what I wrote in my journal:

"There is a huge waterfall. I am looking up at the oceans of water coming over the rim. The water explodes at the bottom, the impact of which creates all kinds of noise, mist and turbulence. The water

spreads over the landscape, completely covering and consuming everything.

"This waterfall is a picture of What Is. I cannot see over the rim. The Source is there but I cannot perceive it. It is infinite and therefore beyond my finite mind to grasp. Immeasurable! The water falling towards the earth is the Incarnation. The What-Is emptied itself and became One with all. The water spreading out over the earth and covering all is what we call Spirit, that has accomplished the purpose of what we call the incarnation, its application and assimilation, manifested in human rights and freedoms."

This changed everything. As I said, up to the night I had this dream, my theological and intellectual life would be described as full of anguish. There was no peace of mind, and my thoughts were conflicting and confusing. My intellect was very dualistic. It was so distressing that I had finally reached the end of my rope. I was so frustrated that I was rapidly approaching the sad conclusion that I would never know the truth, that I would always feel this anguish, and that I would never enjoy peace of mind. I could feel my ministry coming to an end. Even my passion for theology, for spiritual wisdom, was drying up and dying inside. I was ready to completely give up altogether and walk away from it all forever.

Then came the dream. Suddenly!

Some people might argue that the analogy fails because that's all it is, an analogy that diminishes the reality it attempts to represent. But, I'm going to use another analogy to justify this one. Let's take a magnet with a positive and negative pole. No matter how many times it is divided, each piece will still have a positive and negative pole. Even the smallest piece will hold the same properties as the largest. I claim that the waterfall analogy, though small, really is analogous to reality. In fact, it is reality! I would also suggest that this small analogy is a picture of the larger reality I believe it is pointing to, a hidden wholeness and unity that underlies everything though concealed by increasing layers of analogous manifestations.

So, over the ensuing months and years, this dream and the awareness it brought has changed the way I think and do everything. It had a global affect on my life. I didn't know it at the time, but this dream launched the winding down of my ministry as the pastor of my local church. As I've said before, I'd always wrestled with my vocation. But while this dream and this new awareness inspired me to work harder to teach what was true and to help facilitate authentic community, it quickly became apparent that it was not what many people wanted. It was exactly these two areas that mystified, confused, and troubled most of the congregation and many of my readers: my theology and my role as a community facilitator.

But, for me, my theology suddenly found a peaceful place to rest. I came to a place where I knew I didn't know the answers, but this was a place of great serenity, peace, and contentment. Somehow, I understood that even though we seem to believe many differing theologies, philosophies and ideas, that these were only thoughts. Essentially, we are all one, deeply connected, and these different ideas only seem to separate us when in fact they do not. My mind was no longer experiencing confusion, but a kind of fusion, a unitive kind of poise. But it was impossible for me to articulate. I'd read about Bohm that he "believed that the general tendency for individuals, nations, races,

social groups, etc., to see one another as fundamentally different and separate was a major source of conflict in the world. It was his hope that one day people would come to recognize the essential interrelatedness of all things and would join together to build a more holistic and harmonious world." (Michael Talbot, *The Holographic Universe*). I believed this too. In fact, I knew it.

So my messages became even more exploratory and inquisitive. Perhaps even confusing! I understood that we were on a grand search into grasping the mystery together, and the way to do that was through the art of asking open questions. I now understood that questions unlocked the barriers of the mind and that these questions could pull us down into a deeper understanding and appreciation of this mystery. But the mind wants answers. Many religious and spiritual people want to be told how and what to believe. They don't come to a teaching just to leave even more confused than when they came. We are, as the Buddhist Chögyam Trungpa Rinpoche has said, spiritual materialists and consumers looking for anything to substantiate our egos and sense of separateness. This new way of thinking and teaching caused a lot of frustration in the community and it was starting to show.

QUESTIONS ARE THE ANSWER

It seemed that an increasing number of members of my congregation were also getting very frustrated with the way I led. In fact, they would have said that I wasn't leading at all. I admit it was frustrating to me as well, but I felt we were on to something. This dream and my new awareness somehow pulled the rug from under the conventional ways of being a pastor and a leader which are usually expected to manifest authority, strength, and charisma. I was convinced that the best way to function and develop as a healthy community was to contribute to the process collaboratively like a team, like a tribe. In the quantum physicist David Bohm's essay, "On Dialogue and Its Application", he writes:

"Some time ago there was an anthropologist who lived for a long while with a North American tribe. It was a small group of about this size. The hunter-gatherers have typically lived in groups of twenty to forty. Agricultural group units are much larger. Now, from time to time that tribe met like this, in a circle. They just talked and talked and talked, apparently to no purpose. They made no decisions. There was no leader. And everybody could participate. There may have been wise men or wise women who were listened to a bit more – the older ones – but everybody could talk. The meeting went on, until it finally seemed to stop for no reason at all and the group dispersed. Yet

after that, everybody seemed to know what to do, because they understood each other so well. Then they could get together in smaller groups and do something or decide things."

(David Bohm, *On Dialogue*)

So I amplified what I was already doing by experimenting with this style of facilitating community. Even though it was spontaneous, free, and enriching, many believed it was disorganized, chaotic, and fruitless. Just like many go to church to be told what to believe, they also go to experience organized, structured, and programmed fellowship. It takes a lot of energy to be involved in the kind of community I was experimenting with. But most people don't want to work for it. Many want it to be easy … fast, neat and tidy … like fast food at a drive-through. I saw my experiment as potential for a truly healthy, functional, and dynamic community. But many saw it as a recipe for disaster with all these diverse and conflicting ideas, personalities, and agendas. I interpreted this electric engaging of people as fruitful and as the end game itself. But, many saw this endless talking and working with relationships as a fruitless, perpetual and infuriating obstruction to their desires of what a church should be.

I suggest that this is the problem with both arenas … theology and community. Our fantasies of what we think God is gets in the way of What actually is and we will never see It. Our fantasies of what community should be gets in the way of what we actually already are and already have.

Some people started meeting with me to explain that they wondered whether I was suited to be a pastor any more. They felt my teaching had failed. They believed my pastoral gifts had dried up. They questioned my call and my vocation because I was no longer effective.

What I saw as embracing mystery they saw as confusion.

What I saw as facilitating authentic community they saw as a failure to lead.

It was around this time that I received that call from the director of my denomination suggesting that I run my posts by a couple of theologians first to get the stamp of approval or to be edited to a place where they would be safe to post. He was under pressure from the watchdogs of the church and theology. When I got off the phone with him that day, I could see the end was rapidly approaching, and I could feel the noose tightening.

One cold winter's night in March of 2010, I met with a couple of friends who were key supporters in my church. They wanted to speak with me. My wife

wasn't there because she was working. We were having some drinks and talking about the church. It became painfully apparent to me over the course of the evening that they were sharing the same concerns for the church and my leadership that others were. My heart sank. I realized that if I had lost the support of my best friends, then my viability as the pastor was irretrievably gone. The tide had clearly turned against me. They couldn't tell at the time, but I was deeply shaken. I fell into silence. Overcome with defeat, I told them I had to go home. I stepped out into the cold, clear night. The moon was out and shining over the snowy scene before me. I texted Lisa, "I'm done!" She immediately texted back, "Me too!" It was over. Now all that was left was the clean up.

I looked up at the moon and stars and was immediately thrown back to something that happened when I was a teenager. I was walking home from a friend's on a night just like this one. I was overcome with questions, doubt, and fear. I needed reassurance that God was there. I stood before a house that had smoke rising out of its chimney. I prayed, "Dear God, please write your name with that smoke to let me know that you are here!" I waited there for a long time, waiting for God to do a little miracle to assure me of his presence. Nothing. Nothing happened. No name was written with the smoke. No evidence ever came to me that God was there. This night was the same. Just like I knew there

would never be any proof that God was here, neither would I ever receive proof that I was called to be a pastor and continue caring for this congregation. I walked home a finished man.

At the same time though, I felt an immeasurable amount of peace. Theologically I was already at peace. Now I was vocationally at peace. My struggle with my call as a pastor was over. My pastoral vocation had finally breathed its last. I immediately knew what I was going to do. There was a young man in our congregation whom I would recommend to replace me as the pastor. We would have a short time of overlap, but he would take over for me, adopt my incredible leadership team, I would receive a separation package, and then I would leave. The plan was a good one and I would finally be free in just a few weeks.

I had always asked, through my years of questioning my call and whether or not I should continue as a pastor, that it would be clear when it was time for me to quit. I didn't want to run away like a hireling. But I didn't want to stay longer than was healthy for me or for the church. I wanted to know exactly when my perseverance as a pastor collided with the lack of goodwill of the congregation. Tonight was that night. In a moment of lucid clarity I got exactly what I asked for. My time was up. It was over, without a shadow of a doubt. This gave me the assurance that I was doing the right thing.

Just a couple of months before this, Lisa and I took legal advice and filed for personal bankruptcy. My many years serving as a pastor of a church with a growing family and a stay-at-home mom, we had finally come to the point where we were so far in debt that we had no other choice. This was one of my greatest fears all through ministry. I'm not sure why, but it was a fear deeply embedded in my unconscious, so that when it happened I

99

could legitimately quote Job: "That which I greatly feared has come upon me!" I felt guilty, ashamed, unworthy … a complete failure.

So, as I lay on my bed on the night that I said "I quit!" I was suddenly overcome with dread. "What have I done?" I was paralyzed with fear. What was I going to do now? I had a family to support. We had a home. Lisa was still in university studying to be a nurse. I promised her that there would be no drama while she studied, that this was her time and I would protect it with a sacred oath. Now this! We were certainly doomed.

Indeed, my departure transpired just the way I planned it. Within a few weeks I was no longer the pastor of this local congregation.

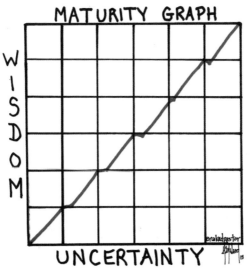

QUESTIONS ARE THE ANSWER

The first Sunday I wasn't a pastor, I went for a walk. It was a sunny spring morning. It was so quiet and peaceful. Some cars drove past and I knew most of them were going to church. I felt so free! It was a delicious feeling and I reveled in it. With my newfound awareness and now my newfound freedom, I predicted that this was how I was going to feel for the rest of my life.

Wrong!

I hadn't even begun my deconstruction. Over the next two years, I would experience another transition through a very dark valley in two different ways.

"To get in you're going to have to bend a little."

It's one thing to have a new awareness. It's another thing to integrate this into one's life, to move from one's head into one's living. I was living a schizophrenic life. I needed theological individuation. I had to learn how to practice what I thought. I had read about Byron Katie's experience: "What I am went so far beyond what my beliefs, at that time, could encompass that I split apart. This is the split we all feel between the manifested self and the real Self. And that can't be put into words either" (A Cry in the Desert: The Awakening of Byron Katie). I couldn't put it into words. I still can't.

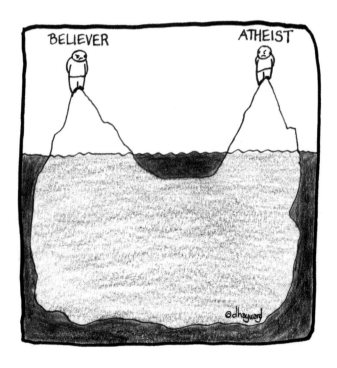

The other area was how to be spiritual. Up to this point, my spirituality presented itself as specifically Christian. I always identified as a Christian, and a professional one at that. I was paid to be an exemplary believer. Now what do I do? Do I just leave the faith and become a kind of churchless agnostic or, worse, as I feared, an atheist? Or do I figure out a new way of being a Christian? I didn't know what to do.

The philosopher Eagleton writes, "What we need is a form of life which is completely pointless, just as the jazz performance is pointless." I loved this quote and applied it to the community life of the church. But, for

my personal life, this didn't feel like a performance, but a noisy cacophony of sound, a bad practice.

For the next five months I lived off of a severance package the church gave me. Actually, this was a very relaxing and enjoyable time. Financially, we were okay because we didn't have any debt and we had enough income to meet our commitments. But as it came time for me to earnestly look for work, something deep within me snapped.

When I was in the ministry, I always felt like I had a purpose. I even felt like I had a destiny. Now that was all wiped away. Now I was a regular person looking for regular work. The feeling I'd always had … that I was

"Take up your questions and follow me."

investing in an important mission or purpose or calling … was gone. I felt no future. Why was I here?

Also, when I was in ministry, I had a keen sense of meaning. Life seemed meaningful because it had purpose and because there was a God who orchestrated it. Now, even though my mind was experiencing a deep residing peace, it was having great difficulty understanding it or integrating this new awareness into everyday life. How could I feel more alive than ever before while life felt less meaningful than ever before? Perhaps Lacan was right when he said, "We attain meaning only at the loss of being." I found being. I lost meaning.

That next September I got a job teaching English as a second language to international university students. I did that for the next two years. I kept up my nakedpastor blog by cartooning and writing every day. At the same time, I launched an online community called The Lasting Supper, where I gather people who are interested, like me, in spiritual independence. I facilitate that community to this day.

But another interesting thing happened during this time. I acquired the help of a spiritual director and psychologist. I had to because Lisa told me to. I wasn't well. I had obviously sunk into a deeply dysfunctional fog

and couldn't find my way out. I was probably depressed. Though my mind was at peace, my life seemed a mess. The incongruity was unbearable. It's a strange period to suffer through because you really do lose your bearings. At one point I felt completely trapped, disconnected, and demoralized. I remember one day considering leaving everything: my wife and family, my home, my blog, and just running away. This was when Lisa insisted I talk to a professional. I did and she helped me walk through my deconstruction without self-destructing. I didn't run.

FREEDOM IS NOT A BIGGER CAGE

Another curious thing happened that helped me. I have been an artist ever since I can remember. In fact, the first story in this book is about my experience drawing as a young boy in church. But my paintings were usually very serene watercolor landscapes. Just after I left the church and was heading into this dark valley I call deconstruction, I found myself drawing with a fine-point pen on paper. I ended up sketching a young girl holding up her teddy bear to a huge grizzly bear towering over her on his haunches. I called it "Fearless". When I showed Lisa, she exclaimed,

"What is THAT?" She knew what it was, but I'd never done anything like that before. Over the next four years I continued drawing this young woman. I called her Sophia, indicating her roots in wisdom, feminism, and Christianity. I completed 59 drawings over the next four years.

Reflecting on it now, I realize it was a kind of personal therapy. Somehow, I was drawing unconscious images of a mysterious process. At the beginning, she finds herself trapped in an abusive and oppressive situation. She escapes and makes her way through her own personal wilderness. Often she is

pictured at night with a full moon, wandering through a lonely land crawling with wild beasts and her own personal struggles. She eventually comes to a place where she recognizes her beauty and divinity and is finally free and walks into the light as a transformed person. I compiled these images and her story into a book, *The Liberation of Sophia*. When I drew the last image, I knew it was finished. My inspiration to draw Sophia evaporated. It was then that I realized that I had not only documented my own journey through deconstruction, but had in a therapeutic way found a way to heal myself and work towards my own wholeness. I faced the questions, didn't settle for an easy answer, and pressed through to a peaceful resolution.

My counselor, my wife Lisa, and my own determination to get whole, helped me to get there, or at least approach it. I eventually came to a much better place.

But it was in my online community The Lasting Supper where I found the perfect combination I needed and had always been looking for. It was the freedom for intellectual inquiry with a safe community space to do it in. And it's working!

There are no perfect churches, just perfect moments. Generally, my years at my last church, though spotted with a number of crises, was a pleasant and largely successful experiment in just this kind of space. I felt very free, even as a pastor, to explore. The box allotted to me for personal theological investigation and authentic community was very generous. But then I met the edges. A box, even though it is very spacious, is still a box. I knew I was no longer willing to comply and fit in. I also knew that, as I've done before, it wouldn't benefit me in the long haul to just move into a bigger box. In fact, I now realized that there is no box. The boxes we construct with all their theological particularities are illusions that give the appearance of separation. I knew we were not separated. We were all one. My deep and serious questions helped me discover that.

Indeed, for me, questions are the answer.

CONCLUSION

*"Always the more beautiful answer
who asks the more difficult question"*
e. e. cummings

One day I was sharing these three stages of questions with an elderly gentleman. He was ninety-two years old, quite fit, living independently, still driving, and interested in talking with me about our journeys. He told me he feels he went through these stages. But, he added, he thinks he came to another stage in his latest years. At first, he seemed to present himself as indifferent, as if he didn't care. I've met many people like this, young and old, who've just given up and don't bother asking questions any more. But deeper into the conversation I realized this old man was at a much deeper place. The surface of things, like a river, is always turbulent. But when you dive deep enough, there is a remarkable calm and serenity. I admired him for continuing his quest until he achieved this level of poise and peace. In fact, he still possessed an inquiring mind. I wondered, since my stages of questioning seem to have been in twenty-five year increments, if I would get to where he is when I turn seventy-five. And, who knows what I will be like when I turn one hundred!

I'll be honest: sometimes I miss the times when things were clear and life was full of certainty. Wittgenstein claimed that this feeling of being "absolutely safe" was paradigmatic of religious experience. I concur!

I came across this quote of José Ortega y Gasset when I was reading Chris Hedges', *Empire of Illusion*:

CONCLUSION

"For the truth is that life on the face of it is a chaos in which one finds oneself lost. The individual suspects as much but is terrified to encounter this frightening reality face to face, and so attempts to conceal it by drawing a curtain of fantasy over it, behind which he can make believe that everything is clear."

Chaos. Lost. Afraid. These aren't endearing words. Unless … unless you are an adventurer, a pilgrim, a pioneer, or an explorer! Then you know they come with the territory. I read Shackleton's call for men to explore with him: "MEN WANTED FOR HAZARDOUS JOURNEY. SMALL WAGES. BITTER COLD. SAFE RETURN DOUBTFUL." I still haven't found what I'm looking for. But will I ever? Do I even want to? I don't want to go back to where I was. I do want to discover. But I also don't want to complete my mission. The joy is in the journey. Actually, the journey is the destination! I'm an explorer, not a settler. This is what I do.

Socrates, when asked what is the right way of life, replied, "Asking after the right way of life … this alone is the right way of life." It used to frustrate the living daylights out of me because I thought the question had to be answered before I could finally live. Now I know Socrates was right. Life is in the question.

Lisa and I have learned in our marriage that in order for our relationship to become richer, we can't think

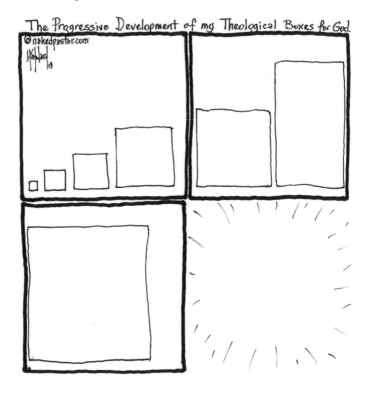

inside the box. We have to think creatively. Like in so many other spheres of life, including church, we tend to think within the paradigm. This not only fortifies old habits, it inhibits new life.

The quantum physicist David Bohm described two kinds of imaginative thinking: one is primary and the other is secondary. Primary imagination is "the direct expression of the creative intent, what we may call the display in the mind. The imagination is the unfoldment of some deeper operation of the mind which is displayed as if coming from the senses, and you can grasp it as if looking at it directly as a whole." Secondary imagination, in contrast, "arises when you keep on repeating an image from the primary display and it becomes automatic."

I don't want to live automatic.

When it comes to living a happy, adventurous life, it requires not secondary imagination because nothing really new can emerge out of this, but only an automatic, habitual and conditioned rearrangement or reenactment of the familiar. Instead, it requires primary imagination where something entirely new can emerge in our minds

and be displayed in our lives. I claim questions, which constantly irritate the status quo, the automatic, and the familiar, are excellent tools for breaking down doors to new ideas. Of course, this must be a perpetual practice because, as in the world of science, every new idea is "falsifiable". That is, it may not be fully true, but only partially so. We can't rest on the laurels of our most recent discoveries. We can enjoy the present. We can be content now, but with the happy awareness that there's always more!

I often compare my spiritual journey to, well, a journey. An exploration. An expedition. I'm not a serious

CONCLUSION

Star Trek fan, but every once in a while I'll hear the phrase going through my mind, "To boldly go where no one has gone before." Indeed, if I am to seek and find, I believe it's going to be a unique journey done uniquely by me on my way to a unique place held uniquely by me.

My life used to be characterized by standing firm on certain beliefs that I would defend like my castle from all attacks. It really was living life from a defensive posture. I used to try to find the answers to the vexing questions in a very neurotic way. My life was full of anxiety and terrible angst. Like Bruce Cockburn's famous line, I would "kick at the darkness 'til it bleeds daylight".

Then the daylight came.

Was the daylight always there and I noticed it when I stopped kicking? Or was kicking at the darkness a necessary stage for me to go through until I could finally see the light? Good question! One that I will probably never stop asking.

But now, even though I'm still searching, it has become a kind of adventure without the attending anxiety. Rather than the energy going into an anxious need to understand, it goes into the adventure of exploring the depths and dimensions of what might benature at the end? true. The search has become the destination rather than the means to it.

Now, there is the freedom to explore, to enter into the mystery, and discover new frontiers.

It is a joyful and exciting way to live. This isn't to say there is never darkness, danger or doldrums. But now I realize these are features of the adventure tour I find myself on. They are part of the package. They are the textures of the tapestry of reality. This is what I expect if I want to press on to a deeper understanding of what is true and into a life of more integrity, joy, and compassion.

I get responses from many people who are alarmed by what they interpret as anger or hatred towards the church or religion in general and Christianity in particular. I get a lot of pity from a lot of people because they feel sorry that I am so full of bitterness and resentment, and that I'm unwilling to forgive, forget and forge ahead.

News flash: I'm one of the happiest people I know. As I hope I've articulated in this book, I know a theological peace I would wish upon everybody. At the same time, I fight endlessly and inexhaustibly for the rights of others to question. Why? Because this is how I finally came to peace. Like I've said, I'm not sure whether my constant questioning got me here or whether it was when I'd finally given up that the peace revealed itself. This is a common question among searchers. But I do know this: people deserve the right to question. I do not mean just by themselves alone in their closets, but also within the communities of which they choose to be members. I believe that churches and all communities would benefit from providing safe spaces for people to explore, journey and discover what is true. So I will continue to critique controlling, toxic, and abusive ideas and behaviors that limit the intellectual curiosity and freedom of people. This really is what nakedpastor is about: fighting for these safe spaces for spiritual inquiry and personal development.

The scientist Gregory Bateson was known to ask "impertinent questions" because he wanted to challenge what he called "the deep epistemological panic" that lurks beneath our obsessive need for certainties. My certainty now is that we live in unfathomable mystery, and it's worth exploring, enjoying, and discovering.

The search is the destination. Questions are the answer.

I would like to share with you a letter I wrote to the members of my online community, The Lasting Supper, that I hope gives a feel for what the journey is like.

Dear Friends,

I compare our journeys to taking a canoe trip down a river.

Sometimes there are rapids where, again, you don't have to paddle. You still have to keep your paddle in the water to avoid damaging your vessel or yourself.

QUESTIONS ARE THE ANSWER

This is a time when things happen very fast and furious. There doesn't seem to be any time to take in the scenery. It's all about survival. I would characterize these times as a mixture of excitement and fear.

Sometimes there are doldrums when nothing at all is happening on its own but requires you to put in all the effort to get anywhere. Everything feels dead. You'd love to enjoy the scenery but you can't just because you're working so hard. Oh, you know you could do nothing and just sit there forever. And sometimes you do. But, realizing you could die here, you put your paddle in the water, engage your muscles, and push yourself forward. I would characterize these times as boring and laborious.

Sometimes there are places you have to portage. This is just plain old hard work where you have to drag your canoe out of the water and carry it with all your gear usually through very rugged terrain. These are the times when you wonder what the heck you're doing out of your environment and sweating bullets and exposing yourself to the wild beasts. I would characterize these times as meaningless and frustrating.

Sometimes you fall in. Either you do something foolish like try to stand up or you hit a rock or a log or water-log the canoe and you're done. It's always an accident.

CONCLUSION

When I took canoe training, one of the things I had to learn was how to right a canoe in water over my head in depth. It's hard work. Then drying everything out. I would characterize these times as dangerous and life-threatening.

Sometimes you are canoeing all alone. No one else is with you and you have no idea if you're doing it right or not. There's no one to talk to. No one to encourage you. No one to listen to your woes or joys. No one who even cares. I would characterize these times as very lonely and discouraging.

Sometimes you're canoeing with another person or two in the same canoe. At times there is fun or deep and meaningful conversation. Other times there are confusing, irritating and annoying exchanges. At times you're glad for the company and other times you'd like to throw them overboard. I would characterize these times as either delightful or aggravating.

I'll tell you how I like to do canoe trips.

I like to have my own canoe, but I like to meet up with other canoeists with their own canoes when I want. This is how I integrate my introverted and extroverted self. Of course, I am aware that sometimes I have no choice in the matter. Sometimes I just find myself very alone. At other times I suddenly find myself surrounded with other canoes.

This is how it feels to me. I feel like we are all in our own canoes making our own trips, but that we have the privilege of meeting up with others who are on the same kind of river. Before, I often felt like I was the only living soul on the whole river. I now know there are many others on the same river and they are my companions. When we collect, and maybe even when we stop and sit around the campfire, we can share our stories and feel reinvigorated for the next day.

What's cool to know though, is that I'm not going nowhere. The river is taking me somewhere. While for me the river is the destination, it is also a way. I'm taking in every minute of it now, but I also feel, deep down, that I'm being taken to a more wonderful place somehow and that I'm going to be a better person for it.

I'm glad you're on the same river with me.

See you at the next campfire!

Happy paddling!

David.

QUESTIONS ARE THE ANSWER

David Hayward's books available on Amazon:

1. *nakedpastor101: Cartoons by David Hayward* (2011). This is David's first book of cartoons. This book contains 101 of his best and most provocative cartoons at the time. There is some text as well.

2. *Without a Vision My People Prosper* (2011). In this book David challenges the modern need to formulate visions and set goals for local congregations. He argues that even though vision and goals might be useful for individuals, businesses and other organizations, it is harmful to genuine community. Through a collection of his most relevant posts and cartoons from his blog, nakedpastor, David passionately endeavors to call the church back to the priority of fellowship over accomplishments.

3. *The Liberation of Sophia* (2014): In 2010, David Hayward underwent a traumatic transition in his life. He began drawing images of a young woman in all kinds of situations. He recognized early on that these drawings weren't just random pictures, but were the articulation of his interior life's journey through spiritual, emotional, intellectual and social transition. He realized that Sophia was him! This is the story of Sophia who starts by finding herself feeling trapped in so many ways. But she won't stay there. This is also the story of her journey into her own independence and freedom. There are 59 drawings, with 59 meditations, that chronicle her journey. Journey with her as she comes face to face with many dangers, but especially with herself. Join with many others who have fallen in love with Sophia and also recognize her story as theirs.

4. *The Art of Coming Out: Cartoons for the LGBTQ Community* (2014): Please note: Many of these cartoons are in color. This book is a collection of cartoons for the LGBTQ community. It is divided into three chapters: the discrimination; the struggle; the affirmation.

David's sites:
1. www.nakedpastor.com (cartoons, art, and posts)
2. www.theLastingSupper.com (his online community)
3. www.nakedpastor.etsy.com (his online shop)
4. You can find David Hayward as the nakedpastor on most social media sites.

You may contact David by email: haywardart@gmail.com